When My Body Gets Big

By Nicole Pigeon

STORY SEED
- PRESS -

When My Body Gets Big
Written by Nicole Pigeon

© 2025 Nicole Pigeon
All rights reserved.

Published by Story Seed Press
Ottawa, Ontario, Canada
Website: www.storyseedpress.com

For permission requests, contact Story Seed Press at:
hello@storyseedpress.com

ISBN: 978-1-997554-12-7, 978-1-997554-13-4, 978-1-997554-14-1

For Élise,

who taught me that big feelings

aren't bad, they're just loud.

Thank you for helping me learn more

about you, more about myself,

and what it means to grow

in patience, in trust,

and in calm—together.

When my body gets big,
and my feelings get loud,
When I can't stop kicking,
When I can't be proud—

I don't need fixing. I don't need shame.
I need your help. I'm not to blame.

My hands are loud.
My heart is fast.
My thoughts are racing,
My calm won't last.

So sit with me. Don't run away.
Please stay close. Help me stay.

Tell me, "You're safe." Tell me, "I'm here."
I need your voice to hold my fear.

I don't need rules. I don't need "No."
I need to feel how far I can go.
Let me push. Let me pull.

Let me cry.
Let me roar.
Then help me come
back to the floor.

Squish my legs.
Rub my back.
Show me where I end.

Give me weight. Give me space.
And remind me: you're my friend.

When I can breathe, and I can hear—
When the storm starts to pass
and the sky becomes clear—

That's when I'll rest. That's when I'll soften.
You held me through the hard.
That matters most often.

My body got big, but you stayed with me.
Now my calm is coming back—quiet as the sea.

And when I wake tomorrow
and the feelings return,
You'll be there again, helping me learn.

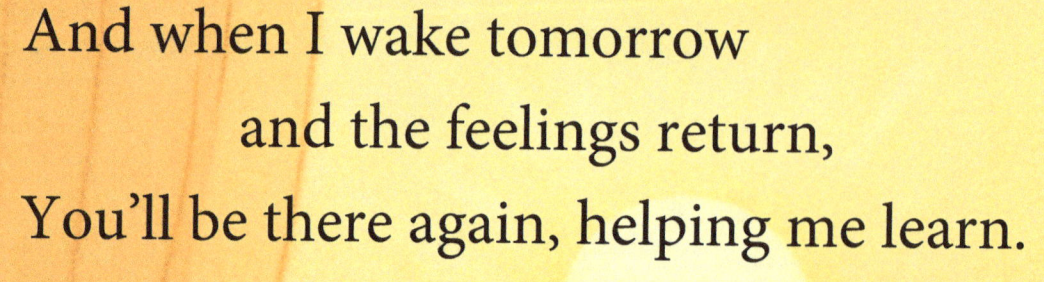

Sensory Actions Glossary

These are the actions mentioned in the book. They're designed to help a dysregulated child feel safe, grounded, and in control of their body again. Each one targets the nervous system, not behavior.

"Squish My Legs"
What it is:
Gently pressing down on the child's legs using your hands, a cushion, or a therapy ball.

Why it helps:
Provides deep pressure input that calms the sensory system and brings body awareness back online.

How to do it:
Ask for permission or offer a choice: "Do you want me to squish your legs like the book?" Use firm, even pressure—not fast or ticklish. Avoid joints—stick to thighs and calves. Stop if your child pulls away or says "no."

"Rub My Back"
What it is:
Slow, rhythmic strokes across the child's back.

Why it helps:
Activates the parasympathetic nervous system (the body's "rest and digest" mode), helping reduce heart rate and anxiety.

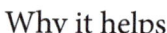

How to do it:
Sit beside or behind the child with consent. Use flat hands and move slowly. Match your breath to the rhythm: slow inhales, slower exhales.

"Show Me Where I End"
What it is:
A phrase to describe helping a child feel the boundaries of their own body using safe, consistent touch.
Why it helps:
Children in sensory overload may feel "floaty" or disconnected from

SHOW ME WHERE I END

their body. This action helps them reestablish body boundaries.

How to do it:
Gently squeeze arms, legs, or shoulders with slow, even pressure. You can use a compression vest, weighted blanket, or wrap them in a blanket ("burrito style") too. "Here are your shoulders. Here are your knees. Here are your toes."

"Give Me Weight"
What it is:
Providing deep pressure input to help the body settle.

Give Me Weight

Why it helps:
Heavy input releases calming chemicals in the brain and reduces sensory defensiveness.

How to do it:
Use a weighted lap pad, stuffy, or blanket. Let the child lay under couch cushions or bean bags if they enjoy that. Sit together with a blanket or pillow over both of you to create shared containment.

"Give Me Space"
What it is:
Honoring a child's need to withdraw without abandoning them.

Why it helps:
Some children regulate better with distance or dim light, but still need connection.

How to do it:
Say, "I'm right here. I'll stay close while you calm your body." Allow them to be in a quiet corner, tent, or under a blanket. Check in gently every few minutes without forcing interaction.

These actions are not one-size-fits-all. They are invitations—not instructions. Always let the child lead. The goal isn't to stop the meltdown, but to help the body come back to safety in a way that honors how it uniquely processes the world.

Dear Grown-Up: How to Use This Book

This is not a behavior book.

It's a co-regulation script—a way to walk with a child through their hardest moments, without shame or punishment.

Children—especially those who are autistic, sensory-sensitive, or emotionally intense—often experience "big body" moments when their nervous systems feel overwhelmed. These moments aren't tantrums. They're dysregulation.

You might see:

Kicking, hitting, or screaming

Running away or shutting down

Refusing all instructions

Fighting bedtime, transitions, or touch

This book gives you a script to speak into the moment—not after it.

How to Use It:

1. During a Meltdown (In-the-Moment Co-Regulation):

Sit with the child, not above or across the room.

Lower your voice. Keep your tone steady and warm.

Read slowly. Use pauses and rhythm like a lullaby.

If they won't let you read it to them, read it near them.

"When my body gets big, and my feelings get loud…"

You are giving their overwhelmed brain a steady, repeatable message:

You're safe. I'm here. I won't abandon you in this storm.

2. As a Bedtime Routine Tool:
   Read it daily before dysregulation.
   Let the repetition become a familiar comfort.

   Discuss it when your child is calm:

   "Remember how the child in the book feels big sometimes? That happens to lots of kids. We can help your body come back down too."

3. As a Visual Model:
   Pair it with calming tools:
   Compression toys or body socks
   Weighted blankets
   Visual timer or calm-down jar
   Squish games, lotion massage, or safe pressure touch

   Let the child choose their preferred regulation tools and link them to moments in the book:
   "Do you want your squish like in the story?"

Why This Matters:
   Children don't learn to calm down because we tell them to.
   They learn to calm down because we co-regulate—again and again—until their nervous system trusts the world enough to settle.
   You don't need perfect words. You need connection, predictability, and patience.
   This book is a tool. You are the medicine.

Big feelings will visit again. That's okay.
When they do, come back to this book.
Read it slowly.
Breathe together.
Feel your body.
Find your calm—together.

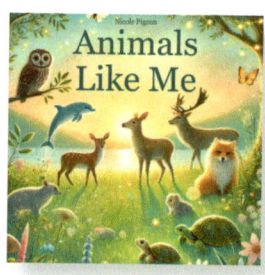   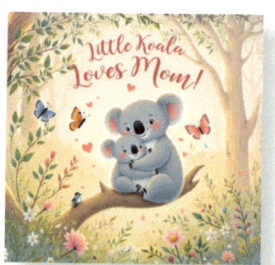

Visit www.storyseedpress.com for updates, activities, and more!

www.ingramcontent.com/pod-product-compliance
Lightning Source LLC
Chambersburg PA
CBHW041502120626
46547CB00003B/512